MARKS&
SPENCER

stir-fry

simple and delicious easy-to-make recipes

Rachael Philipps

Marks and Spencer p.l.c.
Baker Street, London, W1U 8EP

www.marksandspencer.com

ISBN: 1-84273-004-5

Printed in China

Produced by The Bridgewater Book Company Ltd

COVER
Photographer Ian Parsons
Home Economist Sara Hesketh

Acknowledgements
The publishers would like to thank the following
for the use of properties: Louis Potts & Company China Traders, Lewes;
Nakon Interiors, Eastbourne; Steamer Trading Ltd, Lewes; Bright Ideas,
Lewes; Jane Cox, Julie Goodwin, Gareth Mason, Karen Downing and
Daniel Smith for crockery and cutlery from Furniture 151, Lewes.

NOTES FOR THE READER

- This book uses both metric and imperial measurements. Follow the same units of measurement throughout; do not mix metric and imperial.
- All spoon measurements are level: teaspoons are assumed to be 5 ml, and tablespoons are assumed to be 15 ml.
- Unless otherwise stated, milk is assumed to be full fat, eggs and individual vegetables such as potatoes are medium, and pepper is freshly ground black pepper.
- Recipes using raw or very lightly cooked eggs should be avoided by infants, the elderly, pregnant women, convalescents, and anyone suffering from an illness.
- Optional ingredients, variations or serving suggestions have not been included in the calculations. The times given are an approximate guide only. Preparation times differ according to the techniques used by different people and the cooking times may also vary.

contents

introduction

Stir-fries are generally fast, tasty and highly nutritional meals. Only small quantities of meat are used compared with traditional Western cooking, and the healthy emphasis on vegetables, together with accompanying rice and noodles, means they are good for you, too.

Stir-frying is ideal for the busy cook – most recipes are very easy to prepare and quick to cook. And you can be guaranteed to find something in this book to please all tastes, with a wide range of recipes from the Far East, some with Chinese influence and others with spicy Thai and Indian derivation.

The recipes have been divided into four sections – Chicken & Turkey, Fish & Seafood, Beef & Pork, and Vegetables – for ease of reference. You will find that once your confidence grows in this style of cooking, you will enjoy experimenting with ingredients (for example, substituting one kind of meat for another) to suit your own personal tastes.

Stir-frying is a highly versatile and adaptable style of cooking that is great for the bold and imaginative cook. Experiment and enjoy!

guide to recipe key	
easy	Recipes are graded as follows: 1 pea = easy; 2 peas = very easy; 3 peas = extremely easy.
serves 4	Recipes generally serve four people. Simply halve the ingredients to serve two, taking care not to mix imperial and metric measurements.
10 minutes	Preparation time. Where marinating or soaking noodles are involved, these times have been added on separately: eg, 15 minutes + 30 minutes to marinate.
10 minutes	Cooking time. Cooking times don't include the cooking of rice or noodles served with the main dishes.

hot & spicy chicken with peanuts
page 20

ginger prawns with oyster mushrooms
page 28

thai marinated beef with celery
page 66

squash & courgette stir-fry
page 80

chicken
& turkey

Chicken and turkey offer healthy meat options and are very tasty in a wide range of stir-fry dishes – from Curried Turkey with Celery to Chicken with Shiitake Mushrooms. Included in this section are some traditional favourites, such as Chicken Fried Rice, to some more exotic recipes for the bolder cook, such as Turkey with Bamboo Shoots and Water Chestnuts.

curried turkey
with celery

	ingredients	
very easy	1–2 tbsp vegetable oil	1 yellow pepper, sliced thinly
	375 g/13 oz cooked turkey, cubed	1 orange or red pepper, sliced thinly
serves 4	1½ tsp medium curry powder	1 tbsp cornflour
	1 tbsp soy sauce	375 ml/13 fl oz water
	2 leeks, sliced thinly	
	4 celery stalks, chopped finely	2 tbsp chopped coriander, to garnish
10 minutes	225 g/8 oz mangetouts, topped	
	and tailed	cooked noodles or rice, to serve
8 minutes		

Heat a non-stick wok or frying pan and add the oil. Add the turkey, curry powder, soy sauce and leeks and cook for about 2 minutes until the turkey is heated through.

Add the celery, mangetouts and peppers. Stir-fry for another 3–4 minutes.

While the vegetables are cooking, dissolve the cornflour in the water and whisk until well combined. Add the mixture to the stir-fry and cook, stirring constantly until the liquid just thickens.

Remove from the heat, pile over a bed of noodles or rice, garnish with coriander and serve immediately.

turkey, broccoli & pak choi

very easy	
serves 4	
10 minutes + 2 hours to marinate	
9 minutes	

ingredients

MARINADE
1 tbsp soy sauce
1 tbsp honey
2 cloves garlic, crushed

STIR-FRY
450 g/1 lb turkey breast,
    cut into strips
1 tbsp vegetable oil

1 head of broccoli, cut into florets
2 heads of pak choi, leaves washed
    and separated (or savoy cabbage,
    if pak choi is unavailable)
1 red pepper, sliced thinly
50 ml/2 fl oz chicken stock

cooked rice, to serve

In a medium-sized bowl, stir together the soy sauce, honey and garlic. Add the turkey and toss to coat. Cover the bowl with clingfilm and refrigerate for 2 hours to marinate.

Put a wok or large frying pan over a medium-high heat and add the oil; heat for 1 minute. Add the turkey and stir-fry for 3 minutes, or until the turkey is opaque. Remove with a slotted spoon, set aside and keep warm.

Add the broccoli, pak choi (or savoy cabbage) and peppers to the pan and stir-fry for 2 minutes. Add the stock and continue to stir-fry for 2 minutes, or until the vegetables are crisp yet tender.

Return the turkey to the pan and cook briefly to reheat. Serve immediately over a bed of hot rice.

lemon turkey with spinach

	ingredients	
very easy	MARINADE	6 spring onions, sliced finely
	1 tbsp soy sauce	½ lemon, peeled and sliced thinly
serves 4	1 tbsp white wine vinegar	1 garlic clove, chopped finely
	1 tsp cornflour	300 g/10½ oz spinach, washed,
	1 tsp finely grated lemon zest	drained and chopped roughly
12 minutes	½ tsp finely ground black pepper	3 tbsp chopped fresh flat-leaf parsley
+30 minutes		lemon slices, to garnish
to marinate	STIR-FRY	sprigs of flat-leaf parsley, to garnish
	450 g/1 lb turkey breast,	
8 minutes	cut into strips	500 g/1 lb 2 oz cooked tagliatelle or
	1 tbsp vegetable oil	fettucine, to serve

Put the soy sauce, vinegar, cornflour, lemon zest and pepper in a bowl and mix thoroughly. Add the turkey and stir to coat. Cover with clingfilm and marinate in the refrigerator for 30 minutes.

Heat the oil in a large wok or frying pan. Add the turkey and the marinade and cook over a medium heat for 2–3 minutes, or until the turkey is opaque.

Add the spring onions, lemon slivers and garlic and cook for another 2–3 minutes. Stir in the spinach and parsley and cook until the spinach is just wilted.

Remove from the heat, spoon over the hot pasta and garnish with sprigs of parsley and lemon slices before serving.

chicken with pistachio nuts

		ingredients	
very easy		50 ml/2 fl oz chicken stock	450 g/1 lb mushrooms, sliced thinly
		2 tbsp soy sauce	1 head of broccoli, cut into florets
serves 4		2 tbsp dry sherry	150 g/5½ oz beansprouts
		3 tsp cornflour	100 g/3½ oz canned water chestnuts,
		1 egg white, beaten	drained and sliced thinly
15 minutes		½ tsp salt	175 g/6 oz pistachio nuts, plus extra
		4 tbsp peanut or vegetable oil	to garnish (optional)
		450 g/1 lb chicken breast,	
		cut into strips	boiled white rice, to serve
9 minutes			

Combine the chicken stock, soy sauce and sherry with 1 teaspoon of cornflour. Stir well and set aside.

Combine the egg white, salt, 2 tablespoons of the oil and 2 teaspoons of cornflour. Toss and coat the chicken in the mixture.

In a wok or frying pan, heat the remaining vegetable oil until hot. Add the chicken in batches and stir-fry until golden. Remove from the pan, drain on kitchen paper and set aside to keep warm.

Add more oil to the pan if needed and stir-fry the mushrooms, then add the broccoli and cook for 2–3 minutes.

Return the chicken to the pan and add the beansprouts, water chestnuts and pistachio nuts. Stir-fry until all the ingredients are thoroughly warm. Add the chicken stock mixture and cook, stirring continuously until thickened.

Serve immediately over a bed of rice, garnished with pistachios.

ginger chicken with toasted sesame seeds

	ingredients	
extremely easy	MARINADE	2 carrots, sliced thinly
	4 tbsp soy sauce	½ cauliflower, cut into small florets
	4 tbsp water	1 tsp grated fresh root ginger
serves 4		5 tbsp white wine
	STIR-FRY	2 tbsp sesame seeds
10 minutes + 1 hour to marinate	500 g/1 lb 2 oz chicken breasts, skinned, cut into strips	1 tbsp cornflour
		1 tbsp water
	2 tbsp groundnut oil	
	1 leek, sliced thinly	cooked rice, to serve
9 minutes	1 head of broccoli, cut into small florets	

In a medium dish, combine the soy sauce with 4 tablespoons of water. Toss and coat the chicken strips in the sauce. Cover the dish with clingfilm and refrigerate for 1 hour.

Remove the chicken from the marinade with a slotted spoon. Heat the oil in a frying pan or wok, and stir-fry the chicken and leek until the chicken is browned and the leek is beginning to soften.

Stir in the vegetables, ginger and wine. Reduce the heat, cover and simmer for 5 minutes.

Place the sesame seeds on a baking sheet under a hot grill. Stir them once to make sure they toast evenly. Set aside to cool.

In a small bowl, combine the cornflour with 1 tablespoon of water and whisk until smooth. Gradually add the liquid to the frying pan, stirring constantly until thickened.

Pile on a bed of hot rice, top with the sesame seeds and serve.

chicken
& shiitake mushrooms

		ingredients
very easy		
	MARINADE	1 tsp grated fresh root ginger
	175 g/6 oz white sugar	3 carrots, sliced thinly
	225 ml/8 fl oz soy sauce	2 onions, sliced thinly
serves 4	1 tsp Chinese five spice powder	100 g/3½ oz beansprouts
	225 ml/8 fl oz sweet sherry	225 g/8 oz fresh or dried shiitake
		mushrooms, sliced thinly
10 minutes	STIR-FRY	3 tbsp chopped fresh coriander
	2 tbsp vegetable oil	
	675 g/1½ lb chicken breast, skinned	cooked noodles, to serve
10 minutes	and cut into 2.5 cm/1 inch chunks	

Combine the sugar, soy sauce, Chinese five spice powder and sweet sherry in a bowl. Mix well and set aside.

In a frying pan or wok, heat the oil over a medium-high heat. Add the chicken and stir-fry for 2 minutes, then add the ginger and fry for 1 minute, stirring continuously. Add the soy sauce mixture and cook for 2 more minutes.

One at a time add the carrots, onions, beansprouts, mushrooms and coriander. Stir-fry after each addition.

Once the marinade has reduced and is thick, transfer the stir-fry to warm serving bowls. Serve hot with boiled noodles.

hot & spicy chicken
with peanuts

		ingredients	
extremely easy		MARINADE 2 tbsp soy sauce 1 tsp chilli powder (or to taste)	1 tsp grated fresh root ginger 3 shallots, sliced thinly 225 g/8 oz carrots, sliced thinly
serves 4			1 tsp white wine vinegar
		STIR-FRY	pinch of sugar
8 minutes + 30 minutes to marinate		350 g/12 oz chicken breasts, skinned and cut into chunks 4 tbsp peanut oil	90 g/3¼ oz roasted peanuts 1 tbsp groundnut oil
8 minutes		1 clove garlic, chopped finely	cooked noodles, to serve

Mix the soy sauce and chilli powder in a bowl. Add the chicken chunks and toss to coat. Cover with clingfilm and refrigerate for 30 minutes.

Heat the oil in a frying pan or wok, and stir-fry the chicken until browned and well cooked. Remove from the pan, set aside and keep warm.

If necessary, add a little more oil to the pan, then add the garlic, ginger, shallots and carrots. Stir-fry for 2–3 minutes.

Return the chicken to the pan and fry until it is warmed through. Add the vinegar, sugar and peanuts, stir well and drizzle with the groundnut oil.

Serve immediately on a bed of noodles.

chicken fried rice

extremely easy	
serves 4	
12 minutes	
12 minutes	

ingredients

½ tbsp sesame oil
6 shallots, peeled and quartered
450g/1 lb cooked, cubed
  chicken meat
3 tbsp soy sauce
2 carrots, diced

1 stalk celery, diced
1 yellow pepper, diced
175g/6 oz fresh peas
100 g/3½ oz canned sweetcorn
275 g/9½ oz cooked long-grain rice
2 large eggs, scrambled

Heat the oil in a large frying pan over a medium heat. Add the shallots and fry until soft, then add the chicken and 2 tablespoons of the soy sauce and stir-fry for 5–6 minutes.

Stir in the carrots, celery, yellow pepper, peas and sweetcorn and stir-fry for another 5 minutes. Add the rice and stir thoroughly.

Finally, stir in the scrambled eggs and the remaining tablespoon of soy sauce. Serve immediately.

turkey with bamboo shoots & water chestnuts

		ingredients	
very easy		MARINADE	125 g/4½ oz small mushrooms,
		4 tbsp sweet sherry	cut into halves
serves 4		1 tbsp lemon juice	1 green pepper, cut into strips
		1 tbsp soy sauce	1 courgette, sliced thinly
		2 tsp grated fresh root ginger	4 spring onions, cut into quarters
11 minutes + 3–4 hours to marinate		1 clove garlic, crushed	115 g/4 oz canned bamboo shoots, drained
		STIR-FRY	115 g/4 oz canned sliced water
12 minutes		450 g/1 lb turkey breast, cubed	chestnuts, drained
		1 tbsp sesame oil	
		2 tbsp vegetable oil	cooked noodles, to serve

Blend the sherry, lemon juice, soy sauce, ginger and garlic in a bowl, then add the turkey and stir. Cover the dish with clingfilm and refrigerate to marinate for 3–4 hours.

In a wok or frying pan, add the sesame oil and vegetable oil and heat slowly. Remove the chicken from the marinade with a slotted spoon (reserving the marinade) and stir-fry a few pieces at a time until browned. Remove the chicken from the pan and set aside.

Add the mushrooms, green pepper and courgette to the pan and stir-fry for 3 minutes. Add the spring onions and stir-fry for 1 minute more. Add the bamboo shoots and water chestnuts to the pan, then the chicken along with half of the reserved marinade. Stir over a medium-high heat for another 2–3 minutes, until the ingredients are evenly coated and the marinade has reduced.

Serve immediately over noodles or rice.

fish
& seafood

Stir-frying is a great way to prepare fish and seafood because it enhances their delicate texture and subtle flavours. This selection includes spicy options such as Sweet Chilli Squid and Ginger Prawns with Oyster Mushrooms as well as dishes enhanced with herbs, such as Mixed Seafood & Asparagus and Salmon & Scallops with Coriander and Lime – a range of recipes to suit every taste.

ginger prawns
with oyster mushrooms

		ingredients	
very easy		150 ml/5 fl oz chicken stock	3 carrots, sliced thinly
		2 tsp sesame seeds	12 oz oyster mushrooms, sliced thinly
serves 4		3 tsp grated fresh root ginger	1 large red pepper, sliced thinly
		1 tbsp soy sauce	450g/1 lb large prawns, peeled
		¼ tsp hot pepper sauce	2 garlic cloves, crushed
10 minutes		1 tsp cornflour	
		2 tbsp vegetable oil	cooked rice, to serve
10 minutes			

In a small bowl, stir together the chicken stock, sesame seeds, ginger, soy sauce, hot pepper sauce and cornflour until well blended. Set aside.

In a large frying pan or wok, heat 2 tablespoons of the oil. Stir-fry the carrots for 3 minutes, remove from the pan and set aside.

Add 1 tablespoon more oil to the pan and fry the mushrooms for 2 minutes. Remove from the pan and set aside.

Add more oil if needed and stir-fry the pepper with the prawns and garlic for 3 minutes, until the prawns turn pink and opaque.

Stir the sauce again and pour it into the frying pan. Cook until the mixture bubbles, then return the carrots and mushrooms to the pan. Cover and cook for 2 minutes longer, until heated through.

Serve over hot cooked rice.

simple stir-fried scallops

		ingredients	
	extremely easy	SAUCE	STIR-FRY
		2 tbsp lemon juice	450 g/1 lb scallops
		2 tbsp soy sauce	2 tbsp sesame oil
	serves 4	1 tbsp honey	1 tbsp chopped fresh coriander
		1 tbsp minced fresh root ginger	1 tbsp chopped flat-leaf parsley
		1 tbsp fish sauce, optional	
	5 minutes	1 clove garlic, peeled and flattened	rice noodles, to serve
	6 minutes		

Combine the lemon juice, soy sauce, honey, ginger, fish sauce and garlic in a bowl and stir well to dissolve the honey. Add the scallops and toss to coat.

Heat a heavy frying pan or wok over the highest heat for 3 minutes. Add the oil and heat for 30 seconds.

Add the scallops with their sauce and the coriander and parsley to the pan. Stir constantly, cooking for about 3 minutes (less time if the scallops are smaller).

Serve immediately over rice noodles.

prawns, mangetouts & cashew nuts

		ingredients	
very easy		85 g/3 oz dry roasted cashew nuts	450 g/1 lb uncooked prawns, peeled
		3 tbsp peanut oil	1 tsp cornflour
serves 4		4 spring onions, slivered	2 tbsp soy sauce
		2 stalks celery, sliced thinly	50 ml/2 fl oz chicken stock
		3 carrots, sliced finely	225 g/8 oz savoy cabbage, shredded
		100 g/3¾ oz baby corn cobs, halved	175 g/6 oz mangetouts
12 minutes		175 g/6 oz mushrooms, sliced finely	
		1 clove of garlic, chopped roughly	cooked rice, to serve
9 minutes			

Put the frying pan over a medium heat and add the cashew nuts; toast them until they begin to brown. Remove with a slotted spoon and reserve.

Add the oil to the pan and heat. Add the spring onions, celery, carrots and baby corn cobs and cook, stirring occasionally, over a medium-high heat for 3–4 minutes.

Add the mushrooms and cook until they become brown. Mix in the garlic and prawns, stirring until the prawns turn pink.

Mix the cornflour smoothly with the soy sauce and chicken stock. Add the liquid to the shrimp mixture and stir. Then add the savoy cabbage, mangetouts and all but a few of the cashew nuts and cook for 2 minutes.

Garnish with the reserved cashew nuts and serve on a bed of rice.

mixed seafood & asparagus

	ingredients	
easy	MARINADE	225 g/8 oz asparagus,
	4 tbsp sweet sherry	cut into 2.5 cm/1 inch pieces
	1 tsp cornflour	115 g/4 oz baby corn cobs
serves 4		125 ml/4 fl oz chicken stock
	STIR-FRY	2 tbsp sherry
10 minutes	225 g/8 oz prawns, peeled	1 tsp sesame oil
+ 30 minutes	225 g/8 oz tuna,	½ tsp sugar
to marinate	cut into 2.5 cm/1 inch chunks	salt and pepper
	115 g/4 oz squid, sliced into strips	2 tsp cornflour
8 minutes	2 tbsp groundnut oil	5 tsp water
	1 clove garlic, crushed	cooked rice, to serve

To make the marinade mix the sweet sherry and 1 teaspoon of the cornflour together in a large bowl, and season to taste. Add the prawns, tuna and squid to the marinade and mix thoroughly to coat well. Cover with clingfilm and refrigerate for 30 minutes.

Place a frying pan or wok over a high heat until hot. Add the oil, and stir-fry the garlic for about 10 seconds. Remove the seafood from the marinade with a slotted spoon and add to the pan. Stir-fry for 2 minutes, then remove from the pan and set aside.

Add the asparagus, baby corn and stock to the pan; cover and cook for 2 minutes. Add the sherry, sesame oil, sugar, salt and pepper and stir.

Return the seafood to the wok and heat through. Whisk together 2 teaspoons of cornflour and the water. Add to the pan, stirring, until the sauce boils and thickens. Serve on a bed of rice.

monkfish stir-fry

extremely easy	
serves 4	
10 minutes	
5 minutes	

ingredients

2 tsp sesame oil
450 g/1 lb monkfish steaks,
    cut into 2.5 cm/1 inch chunks
1 onion, sliced thinly
3 cloves garlic, chopped finely
1 tsp grated fresh ginger root
225 g/8 oz fine tip asparagus

175 g/6 oz mushrooms, sliced thinly
2 tbsp soy sauce
1 tbsp lemon juice

lemon wedges, to garnish

cooked noodles, to serve

Heat the oil in a frying pan over a medium-high heat. Add the fish, onion, garlic, ginger, asparagus and mushrooms. Stir-fry for 2–3 minutes.

Stir in the soy sauce and lemon juice and cook for another minute. Remove from the heat and transfer to warm serving dishes.

Garnish with lemon wedges and serve immediately on a bed of cooked noodles.

sweet chilli squid

extremely easy	
serves 4	
10 minutes	
7 minutes	

ingredients

1 tbsp sesame seeds, toasted	4 tbsp soy sauce
2 tbsp sesame oil	1 tsp sugar
280 g/10 oz squid, cut into strips	1 tsp hot chilli flakes, or to taste
2 red peppers, sliced thinly	1 clove of garlic, crushed
3 shallots, sliced thinly	1 tsp sesame oil
85 g/3 oz mushrooms, sliced thinly	
1 tbsp dry sherry	cooked rice, to serve

Place the sesame seeds on a baking sheet, toast under a hot grill and set aside. Heat 1 tablespoon of oil in a frying pan over a medium heat. Add the squid and cook for 2 minutes. Remove from the pan and set aside.

Add the other tablespoon of oil to the pan and fry the peppers and shallots over a medium heat for 1 minute. Add the mushrooms and fry for another 2 minutes.

Return the squid to the pan and add the sherry, soy sauce, sugar, chilli flakes and garlic, stirring thoroughly. Cook for a further 2 minutes.

Sprinkle with the toasted sesame seeds, drizzle over the sesame oil and mix. Serve on a bed of rice.

salmon & scallops
with coriander & lime

	ingredients	
very easy	6 tbsp groundnut oil	1 clove garlic, crushed
	280 g/10 oz salmon steak, skinned	6 tbsp chopped fresh coriander
	and cut into 2.5 cm/1 inch chunks	3 shallots, sliced thinly
serves 4	225 g/8 oz scallops	2 limes, juiced
	3 carrots, sliced thinly	1 tsp lime zest
	2 celery stalks, cut into	1 tsp dried red pepper flakes
12 minutes	2.5 cm/1 inch pieces	3 tbsp dry sherry
	2 orange peppers, sliced thinly	3 tbsp soy sauce
	175 g/6 oz oyster mushrooms,	
8 minutes	sliced thinly	cooked noodles, to serve

In a large frying pan or wok, heat the oil over a medium heat. Add the salmon and scallops, and stir-fry for 3 minutes. Remove from the pan, set aside and keep warm.

Add the carrots, celery, peppers, mushrooms and garlic to the pan and stir-fry for 3 minutes. Add the coriander and shallots, and stir.

Add the lime juice and zest, dried red pepper flakes, sherry and soy sauce and stir. Return the salmon and scallops to the pan and stir-fry carefully for another minute.

Serve immediately on a bed of cooked noodles.

beef
& pork

Stir-frying beef and pork is one of the quickest ways of cooking these meats – and one of the tastiest and healthiest, too. If you favour Thai flavours, you can choose Thai Marinated Beef with Celery. If you prefer, you can choose Chinese dishes, such as Szechuan-style Pork & Pepper or Chinese-style Marinated Beef with Vegetables. But whatever your taste, there's something here for everyone.

beef & peanuts
with vegetables

		ingredients	
very easy		MARINADE	1 clove garlic, crushed
		1 tsp cornflour	½ cup water
serves 4		1 tbsp soy sauce	2 tbsp groundnut oil
		1 tsp grated fresh root ginger	4 spring onions, sliced thinly
			115 g/4 oz baby corn cobs, halved
8 minutes +20 minutes to marinate		STIR-FRY	1 carrot, sliced thinly
		450 g/1 lb rump steak, cut into thin strips	90 g/3¼ oz roasted peanuts
6 minutes		1 tsp cornflour	fresh coriander, to garnish
		1 tbsp soy sauce	
		2 tsp white wine vinegar	cooked rice, to serve

To make the marinade, mix together the cornflour, soy sauce and ginger in a medium bowl. Add the beef strips and toss to coat well. Cover with clingfilm and leave to marinate for 20 minutes.

In a small bowl, mix 1 teaspoon of cornflour with 1 tablespoon of soy sauce, the wine vinegar, garlic and the water and set aside.

In a frying pan or wok, heat 1 tablespoon of oil over a medium heat. Stir-fry the beef for 2 minutes, remove and set aside.

Using the same pan, heat the remaining oil, add the spring onions, corn cobs and carrots and stir-fry for 2 minutes. Stir in the beef and soy sauce mixture and bring to the boil. When the stir-fry thickens, add the peanuts. Transfer the stir-fry to warm serving dishes and garnish with fresh coriander. Serve on a bed of rice.

pork with basil & lemongrass

		ingredients
very easy	MARINADE	1 courgette, sliced thinly
	1 stalk lemon grass, sliced finely	2 carrots, sliced thinly
serves 4	2 tbsp fish sauce, optional	115 g/4 oz canned bamboo shoots
	4 tbsp fresh basil, shredded	115 g/4 oz canned water chestnuts,
	juice of 1 lime	sliced thinly
12 minutes		1 garlic clove, crushed
+ 1–2 hours	STIR-FRY	125 ml/4 fl oz chicken stock
to marinate	350 g/12 oz pork tenderloin, cubed	
	2 tbsp sesame oil	wedges of lime, to garnish
12 minutes	280 g/10 oz mushrooms, sliced thinly	cooked basmati rice, to serve

Mix the lemongrass, fish sauce (if desired), basil and lime juice in a bowl. Stir in the pork and toss well to coat. Cover with clingfilm and refrigerate for 1–2 hours.

Heat 1 tablespoon of the oil in a frying pan or wok over a medium heat. Add the meat and the marinade and stir-fry until the pork is browned. Remove from the pan, set aside and keep warm.

Add the remaining 1 tablespoon of oil to the pan and heat. Add all the vegetables and the garlic and stir-fry for about 3 minutes.

Return the pork to the pan and add the chicken stock. Cook for 5 minutes until the stock is reduced.

Transfer the stir-fry to warm serving dishes and garnish with wedges of lime. Serve on a bed of basmati rice.

hot & spicy beef
with toasted pine nuts

		ingredients	
very easy	MARINADE	2 tbsp white wine vinegar	
	2 tbsp soy sauce	1 tsp cornflour	
serves 4	1 tbsp cornflour	2 tbsp groundnut oil	
	1 tbsp water	3 tsp grated fresh root ginger	
		2 red, hot chillis, chopped finely	
10 minutes	STIR-FRY	1 leek, sliced thinly	
+ 1 hour	450 g/1 lb rump steak,	2 carrots, sliced thinly	
to marinate	cut into thin strips	100 g/3½ oz fine tip asparagus	
	55 g/2 oz pine nuts	3 shallots, sliced thinly	
12 minutes	1 lime, juiced		
	1 tbsp soy sauce	cooked noodles, to serve	

To make the marinade, mix the soy sauce with the cornflour and water in a medium bowl. Add the beef and stir until the meat is well coated. Cover the bowl with clingfilm and chill in the refrigerator for 1 hour. Spread the pine nuts on a baking sheet and toast under a grill.

Mix the lime juice, the soy sauce, the vinegar, cornflour and 1 tablespoon of the groundnut oil in a small bowl and set aside. Heat the remaining groundnut oil in a large frying pan or wok. Stir-fry the ginger, chilli peppers and leek for 2 minutes. Add the beef and the marinade and stir-fry for a further minute.

Stir in the carrots, asparagus and shallots and fry for 7 minutes or until the beef is cooked through. Add the lime mixture, reduce the heat and simmer until the liquid thickens. Remove from the heat, sprinkle with the pine nuts and serve.

quick pork &
pasta stir-fry

extremely easy	
serves 4	
8 minutes	
8 minutes	

ingredients

1 tbsp groundnut oil
½ tsp chilli powder, or to taste
2 garlic cloves, crushed
½ red cabbage, shredded
2 leeks, sliced thinly
1 orange pepper, sliced thinly

1 carrot, sliced thinly
1 courgette, sliced thinly
350 g/12 oz pork tenderloin, cubed

cooked fettucine or vermicelli, to serve

Heat the oil in a large frying pan or wok over a medium heat and add the chilli powder, garlic and red cabbage. Stir-fry for 2–3 minutes.

Stir in the rest of the vegetables and cook for a further 2 minutes. Add the meat, increase the heat and stir-fry for about 5 minutes, or until the pork is well cooked and the dish is piping hot.

Serve immediately over fettucine or vermicelli.

szechuan-style pork & pepper

	ingredients	
very easy	MARINADE	250 ml/9 fl oz water
	1 tbsp soy sauce	2 tbsp groundnut oil
serves 4	pinch of chilli flakes	2 leeks, sliced thinly
		1 red pepper, cut into thin strips
	STIR-FRY	1 courgette, cut into thin strips
10 minutes	500 g/1 lb 2 oz pork tenderloin, cubed	1 carrot, cut into thin strips
+ 30 minutes to marinate	2 tbsp cornflour	pinch of salt
	3 tbsp soy sauce	
	1 tbsp white wine vinegar	cooked wild rice, to serve
12 minutes		

To make the marinade, mix the soy sauce and chilli flakes in a bowl. Add the pork cubes and toss to coat. Cover with clingfilm and leave to stand for 30 minutes.

Combine the cornflour, soy sauce and white wine vinegar in a small bowl. Stir in the water gradually, then set aside.

Heat 1 tablespoon of the oil in a wok or frying pan. Add the pork and marinade mixture and stir-fry for 2–3 minutes. Remove the pork from the pan with a slotted spoon and set aside.

Heat the remaining oil in the pan, add the leeks and red pepper and stir-fry for 2 minutes. Then add the courgette, carrot and salt and stir-fry for 2 more minutes.

Stir in the pork and the cornflour mixture and bring to the boil, stirring constantly until the sauce thickens. Remove from the heat.

Serve immediately over cooked wild rice.

ginger beef with
yellow peppers

extremely easy	
serves 4	
10 minutes +30 minutes to marinate	
9 minutes	

ingredients

MARINADE
2 tbsp soy sauce
2 tsp groundnut oil
1½ tsp caster sugar
1 tsp cornflour

STIR-FRY
500 g/1 lb 2 oz beef fillet,
   cut into 2.5 cm/1 inch cubes
2 tsp groundnut oil

2 garlic cloves, crushed
2 tbsp grated fresh root ginger
pinch of chilli flakes
2 yellow peppers, sliced thinly
125 g/4½ oz baby corn
175 g/6 oz mangetouts

hot noodles drizzled with sesame oil,
   to serve

To make the marinade, mix the soy sauce, groundnut oil, sugar and cornflour in a bowl. Stir in the beef cubes, then cover with clingfilm and set aside to marinate for 30 minutes.

Heat the groundnut oil in a frying pan or wok over a medium heat. Add the garlic, ginger and chilli flakes and cook for 30 seconds.Stir in the yellow peppers and baby corn, and stir-fry for 2 minutes. Add the mangetouts and cook for another minute.

Remove the vegetables from the pan. Put the beef cubes and marinade into the pan and stir-fry for 3–4 minutes or until cooked to taste. Return the vegetables to the pan, mix well and cook until all the ingredients are heated through.

Remove from the heat and serve over noodles.

chinese-style marinated beef with vegetables

		ingredients	
easy		MARINADE	3 tbsp sesame oil
		1 tbsp dry sherry	½ tbsp soy sauce
serves 4		½ tbsp soy sauce	½ tbsp cornflour
		½ tbsp cornflour	3 tbsp sesame oil
		½ tsp caster sugar	1 head of broccoli, cut into florets
12 minutes +30 minutes to marinate		2 garlic cloves, chopped finely	2 carrots, cut into thin strips
		1 tbsp sesame oil	125 g/4 oz mangetouts
			125 ml/4 fl oz beef stock
6 minutes		STIR-FRY	250 g/9 oz baby spinach, shredded
		500 g/1 lb 2 oz rump steak,	fresh coriander, to garnish
		cut into thin strips	cooked white rice or noodles, to serve

To make the marinade, mix the sherry, soy sauce, cornflour, sugar, garlic and sesame oil in a bowl. Add the beef to the mixture, cover with clingfilm and set aside to marinate for 30 minutes.

Heat 1 tablespoon of the sesame oil in a frying pan or wok. Stir-fry the beef without its marinade for 2 minutes until medium-rare. Discard the marinade. Remove the beef from the pan and set aside.

Combine the cornflour and soy sauce in a bowl and set aside. Pour the remaining 2 tablespoons of sesame oil into the pan, add the broccoli, carrots and mangetouts and stir-fry for 2 minutes.

Add the stock, cover the pan and steam for one minute. Stir in the spinach, beef and the cornflour mixture. Cook until the juices boil and thicken.

Serve over white rice or noodles and garnish with fresh coriander.

hot sesame beef

very easy	
serves 4	
10 minutes	
10 minutes	

ingredients

500 g/1 lb 2 oz beef fillet,
  cut into thin strips
1½ tbsp sesame seeds
125 ml/4 fl oz beef stock
2 tbsp soy sauce
2 tbsp grated fresh root ginger
2 garlic cloves, chopped finely
1 tsp cornflour
½ tsp chilli flakes
3 tbsp sesame oil

1 large head of broccoli,
  cut into florets
1 orange pepper, sliced thinly
1 red chilli, deseeded and sliced finely
1 tbsp chilli oil, to taste

1 tbsp chopped fresh coriander,
  to garnish

cooked wild rice, to serve

Mix the beef strips with 1 tablespoon of the sesame seeds in a small bowl. In a separate bowl, whisk together the beef stock, soy sauce, ginger, garlic, cornflour and chilli flakes.

Heat 1 tablespoon of the sesame oil in a large frying pan or wok. Stir-fry the beef strips for 2–3 minutes. Remove and set aside.

Discard any remaining oil in the pan, then wipe with kitchen paper to remove any stray sesame seeds. Heat the remaining oil, add the broccoli, orange pepper, chilli and chilli oil (if desired) and stir-fry for 2–3 minutes. Stir in the beef stock mixture, cover and simmer for 2 minutes.

Return the beef to the pan and simmer until the juices thicken, stirring occasionally. Cook for another 1–2 minutes.

Sprinkle with the remaining sesame seeds. Serve over cooked wild rice and garnish with fresh coriander.

beef with cashew nuts

easy	
serves 4	
12 minutes	
9 minutes	

ingredients

4 tbsp groundnut oil
500 g/1 lb 2 oz beef fillet,
  cut into 2.5 cm/1 inch cubes
8 spring onions, trimmed and sliced
2 carrots, cut into thin strips
8 radishes, sliced thinly
2 garlic cloves, chopped finely
2 tbsp grated fresh root ginger
90 g/3¼ oz cashew nuts
125 ml/4 fl oz water
4 tsp cornflour

4 tsp soy sauce
1 tsp sesame oil
1 tbsp oyster sauce
1 tsp chilli sauce

GARNISH
2 tbsp cashew nuts
1 tbsp chopped coriander

cooked noodles or rice, to serve

In a frying pan or wok, heat 2 tablespoons of the groundnut oil and stir-fry the beef cubes for 3–4 minutes. Cooking the meat in batches can help to speed up the process. Remove the cooked meat from the pan and set aside.

Heat the remaining 2 tablespoons of groundnut oil in the pan and stir-fry the spring onions, carrots, radishes, garlic, ginger and cashew nuts for 1–2 minutes.

Mix the water, cornflour, soy sauce, sesame oil, oyster sauce and chilli sauce in a small jug or bowl and set aside.

Return the beef to the pan and stir-fry until hot; then pour the cornflour mixture into the pan. Cook gently, stirring constantly until the sauce boils and thickens.

Remove from the heat, pile on top of the rice or noodles, and garnish with cashew nuts and coriander.

beef & black
bean sauce

extremely easy	
serves 4	
12 minutes +30 minutes to marinate	
12 minutes	

ingredients

MARINADE
1 tbsp soy sauce
1 tbsp dry sherry
2 tbsp water
1 tbsp cornflour

SAUCE
2 tbsp black bean sauce
1 tbsp soy sauce
1 tbsp dry sherry
1 tbsp cornflour

STIR-FRY
375 g/13 oz rump steak, cubed
6 tbsp vegetable oil
4 cloves garlic, chopped finely
1 tbsp grated fresh root ginger
2 leeks, sliced thinly
1 head of broccoli, cut into florets
1 head of cauliflower, cut into florets
4 tbsp water

cooked noodles or rice, to serve

To make the marinade, combine the soy sauce, sherry, water and cornflour in a bowl. Add the cubes of beef, stir to coat well and set aside to marinate for 30 minutes. In a separate bowl, mix the sauce ingredients together.

In a frying pan or wok, heat 4 tablespoons of the oil and stir-fry the beef for 3–4 minutes. Remove from the pan and set aside.

Wipe the pan clean with kitchen paper. Heat the remaining oil, and stir-fry the garlic, ginger and leeks for 1 minute. Add the broccoli, cauliflower and water. Reduce the heat, cover the pan and simmer for 3–4 minutes.

Return the beef to the pan and stir well. Pour the sauce into the pan and bring to the boil. Reduce the heat, and simmer for 4–5 minutes until the sauce is thick and the ingredients are cooked to your liking. Serve over cooked noodles or rice.

marinated steak
with rice noodles

		ingredients	
easy		MARINADE	STIR-FRY
		1 tsp dry sherry	280 g/10 oz rump steak, cut into strips
		1 tbsp soy sauce	300 ml/10 fl oz vegetable oil,
serves 4		1 tbsp groundnut oil	to deep-fry noodles
		1 tsp sesame oil	225 g/9 oz rice noodles
8 minutes		1 tsp cornflour	1 tbsp soy sauce
+ 1 hour		2 tsp honey	1 tbsp black bean sauce
to marinate		1 shallot, chopped finely	1 tsp cornflour
			125 ml/4 fl oz water
8 minutes			8 spring onions, sliced thinly
			fresh coriander, to garnish

For the marinade, mix the sherry, soy sauce, groundnut oil, sesame oil, cornflour, honey and shallot in a large bowl. Add the beef and toss to coat. Cover with clingfilm and refrigerate for 1 hour.

In a frying pan or wok, heat the oil over a high heat until very hot. Using a metal sieve, lower the noodles into the oil for 3 seconds until they are puffed up. Remove carefully, let the oil drain from the sieve and set the noodles aside to cool on kitchen paper. Snap the cooled noodles into smaller lengths and set aside.

Take 5 tablespoons of oil from the pan and heat in a second frying pan or wok. Stir-fry the beef over a medium heat for 3–4 minutes. Remove from the pan and set aside. Add the soy sauce, black bean sauce, cornflour and water to the oil in the second pan and cook gently until the mixture boils. Add the spring onions and beef and cook for 1 minute. Remove from the heat and serve over the noodles. Garnish with coriander.

thai marinated beef
with celery

	ingredients	
extremely easy	MARINADE	1 red pepper, cut into thin strips
	1 tsp salt	1 red chilli, seeds removed,
	2 tbsp fish sauce	sliced finely
serves 4		250 ml/9 fl oz vegetable oil
	STIR-FRY	
10 minutes + 1 hour to marinate	500 g/1 lb 2 oz beef fillet, cut into thin strips	cooked rice noodles drizzled with sesame oil, to serve
	3 celery stalks, cut into 2.5 cm/1 inch batons	
6 minutes		

To make the marinade, mix the salt and fish sauce in a large bowl. Add the beef and toss to coat. Cover with clingfilm and put in the refrigerator for 1 hour to marinate.

Heat the oil in the pan and deep-fry the beef over a medium heat for 2–3 minutes until crispy. Remove the pan from the heat and, using a slotted spoon, lift out the meat and drain it on kitchen paper. Discard all but 2 tablespoons of the oil.

Heat the remaining oil in the pan and stir-fry the celery, red pepper and chilli for 1 minute. Add the beef and cook until hot.

Serve over noodles drizzled with sesame oil.

stir-fry solo

easy	
serves 1	
10 minutes + 30 minutes to marinate	
8 minutes	

ingredients

MARINADE
1 tsp cornflour
2 tbsp dry sherry

STIR-FRY
125 g/4½ oz chicken breast,
  cut into thin strips
2 tsp sesame oil
2 garlic cloves, crushed
1 tsp grated fresh root ginger

1 small head of broccoli,
  cut into florets
1 stalk of celery, cut into batons
1 carrot, cut into batons
¼ orange pepper, sliced thinly
2 tbsp soy sauce

1 tbsp chopped fresh coriander,
  to garnish
cooked rice, to serve

To make the marinade, combine the cornflour and dry sherry in a bowl. Add the chicken, tossing well to coat. Cover with clingfilm and allow to marinate in the refrigerator for 30 minutes.

Put the oil in a large frying pan or wok and heat over a high heat. Add the garlic, ginger and chicken and cook for 3 minutes.

Add the broccoli, celery, carrot and pepper to the pan and cook for 3 minutes, stirring constantly. Add more oil if necessary to prevent the dish drying out. Stir in the soy sauce and cook for another minute.

Serve piled on a bed of rice and garnished with the coriander.

pad thai
(thai fried noodles)

	ingredients		
easy	225 g/9 oz rice noodles	vegetable oil,	175 g/6 oz prawns, peeled,
	90 g/3¼ oz peanuts,	for deep frying	cut in half lengthways
serves 4	chopped roughly	3 tbsp peanut oil	3 eggs, beaten
	2 tbsp lime juice	1 garlic clove, crushed	
	1 tbsp caster sugar	1 onion, sliced finely	GARNISH
15 minutes	6 tbsp fish sauce	1 red pepper, sliced thinly	1 lemon, cut into wedges
+20 minutes to soak noodles	1 tsp hot chilli sauce, or to taste	250 g/9 oz chicken breast, cut into thin strips	4 spring onions, chopped finely
	250 g/9 oz firm tofu,	90 g/3 oz beansprouts	2 tbsp chopped peanuts
14 minutes	cubed	125 g/4½ oz mangetouts	1 tbsp chopped fresh basil

Soak the noodles in a bowl of warm water for about 20 minutes, or until soft. Drain thoroughly in a colander and set aside. In a small bowl, combine the peanuts, lime juice, sugar, fish sauce and hot chilli sauce and set aside.

Rinse the tofu in cold water, place between layers of kitchen paper and pat dry. Heat the oil for deep-frying in a large frying pan or wok. Deep-fry the tofu over a medium heat for 2 minutes until light brown and crisp. Remove from the heat, lift tofu out with a slotted spoon and set aside on kitchen paper to drain.

Heat a large frying pan or wok and add the peanut oil, garlic, onion, red pepper and chicken strips. Cook for 2–3 minutes. Stir in the beansprouts and mangetouts and cook for 1 minute. Then add the prawns, noodles, eggs and tofu and stir-fry for 4–5 minutes. Finally, add the peanut and lime juice mixture and cook for 3–4 minutes. Transfer to warm dishes, garnish and serve.

vegetable dishes

Vegetables retain their crunchy freshness when they are stir-fried, and their natural healthy taste can be quickly enhanced with delicious simple and exotic sauces.

From Oyster Mushrooms & Vegetables with Peanut Chilli Sauce and Spicy Indian Vegetarian Stir-fry through to Meatless Pad Thai, there is a great selection of main and side dishes here to tantalise all taste buds.

oyster mushrooms & vegetables with peanut chilli sauce

		ingredients	
very easy		1 tbsp sesame oil	2 tbsp coarse peanut butter
		4 spring onions, sliced finely	1 tsp chilli powder, or to taste
serves 4		1 carrot, cut into batons	3 tbsp water
		1 courgette, cut into batons	
		½ head of broccoli,	wedges of lime, to garnish
		cut into florets	
10 minutes		450 g/1 lb oyster mushrooms,	cooked rice or noodles, to serve
		sliced thinly	
6 minutes			

Heat the oil in a frying pan or wok until almost smoking. Stir-fry the spring onions for 1 minute. Add the carrot and courgette and stir-fry for another minute. Then add the broccoli and cook for one more minute.

Stir in the mushrooms and cook until they are soft and at least half the liquid they produce has evaporated. Add the peanut butter and stir well. Season with the chilli powder to taste. Finally, add the water and cook for a further minute.

Serve over rice or noodles and garnish with wedges of lime.

spicy indian vegetarian stir-fry

	ingredients	
very easy	3 tbsp vegetable oil	¼ tsp chilli powder
	½ tsp turmeric	4 tomatoes, chopped roughly
serves 4	225 g/8 oz potatoes,	300 g/10½ oz spinach (de-stalked),
	cut into 1 cm/½ inch cubes	chopped roughly
	3 shallots, chopped finely	125 g/4½ oz fresh or frozen peas
	1 bay leaf	1 tbsp lemon juice
10 minutes	½ tsp ground cumin	salt and pepper
	1 tsp finely grated fresh	
	root ginger	cooked basmati rice, to serve
15 minutes		

In a large frying pan or wok, heat 2 tablespoons of the oil and add the turmeric and a pinch of salt. Carefully add the potatoes, stirring continuously to coat in the turmeric. Stir-fry for 5 minutes, remove from the pan and set aside.

Heat the remaining tablespoon of oil and stir-fry the shallots for 1–2 minutes. Mix in the bay leaf, cumin, ginger and chilli powder, then add the tomatoes and stir-fry for two minutes.

Add the spinach, mixing well to combine all the flavours. Cover and simmer for 2–3 minutes. Return the potatoes to the pan and add the peas and lemon juice. Cook for 5 minutes or until the potatoes are tender.

Remove the pan from the heat, discard the bay leaf and season with salt and pepper. Serve with cooked basmati rice.

classic stir-fried vegetables

very easy	
serves 4	
10 minutes	
6 minutes	

ingredients

3 tbsp sesame oil
8 spring onions, chopped finely
1 garlic clove, crushed
1 tbsp grated fresh root ginger
1 head of broccoli, cut into florets
1 orange or yellow pepper,
  chopped roughly
125 g/4½ oz red cabbage, shredded
125 g/4½ oz baby sweetcorn

175 g/6 oz portobello or large cup
  mushrooms, sliced thinly
200 g/7 oz fresh beansprouts
250 g/9 oz canned water chestnuts,
  drained
4 tsp soy sauce

cooked wild rice, to serve

Heat 2 tablespoons of the oil in a large frying pan or wok over a high heat. Stir-fry six of the spring onions, with the garlic and ginger for 30 seconds.

Add the broccoli, pepper and red cabbage and stir-fry for 1–2 minutes. Mix in the baby sweetcorn and mushrooms and stir-fry for a further 1–2 minutes.

Finally, add the beansprouts and water chestnuts and cook for another 2 minutes. Pour in the soy sauce to taste and stir well.

Transfer to warm dishes and serve immediately over cooked wild rice, and garnish with spring onions.

squash & courgette stir-fry

	ingredients	
very easy	1 butternut squash, peeled, deseeded and cut into 2.5 cm/1 inch cubes	¼ small cauliflower, cut into florets
serves 4	2 tbsp olive oil	1 tsp chopped fresh basil
	2 tbsp vegetable oil	½ tsp dried oregano
	2 cloves of garlic, crushed	4 tbsp dry white wine
	1 carrot, sliced thinly	1 tbsp chopped fresh coriander
12 minutes	2 green or yellow courgettes, sliced thinly on the diagonal	1 tbsp lemon juice
35 minutes	1 small head of broccoli, cut into florets	cooked noodles, to serve

Preheat the oven to 180°C/350°F/Gas Mark 4. Place the butternut squash in an ovenproof dish, drizzle with the olive oil and season generously. Bake for 20–30 minutes until firm but tender. Insert a knife into a squash cube to test for tenderness. Remove from the oven and set aside.

Heat the vegetable oil in a large frying pan or wok. Add the garlic and cook for 30 seconds, then add the carrot, courgettes, broccoli and cauliflower. Stir-fry for 1 minute and then add the squash.

Add the basil, oregano and wine. Cover the pan and simmer for 3–4 minutes. Remove from the heat. Add the coriander and the lemon juice. Serve immediately over cooked noodles.

spicy tofu

	ingredients	
very easy	**MARINADE**	4 tbsp groundnut oil
	75 ml/2½ fl oz vegetable stock	1 tbsp grated fresh root ginger
serves 4	2 tsp cornflour	3 garlic cloves, crushed
	2 tbsp soy sauce	4 spring onions, sliced thinly
	1 tbsp caster sugar	1 head of broccoli, cut into florets
10 minutes	pinch of chilli flakes	1 carrot, cut into batons
+20 minutes		1 yellow pepper, sliced thinly
to marinate	**STIR-FRY**	250 g/9 oz shiitake mushrooms,
	250 g/9 oz firm tofu, rinsed and	sliced thinly
10 minutes	drained thoroughly and cut into	steamed rice, to serve
	1 cm/½ inch cubes	

Blend the vegetable stock, cornflour, soy sauce, sugar and chilli
flakes together in a large bowl. Add the tofu and toss well to
cover in the marinade. Set aside to marinate for 20 minutes.

In a large frying pan or wok, heat 2 tablespoons of the groundnut
oil and stir-fry the tofu with its marinade until brown and crispy.
Remove from the pan and set aside.

Heat the remaining 2 tablespoons of groundnut oil in the pan and
stir-fry the ginger, garlic and spring onions for 30 seconds. Add
the broccoli, carrot, yellow pepper and mushrooms to the pan and
cook for 5–6 minutes. Return the tofu to the pan and stir-fry to
reheat. Serve immediately over steamed rice.

meatless pad thai (thai fried noodles)

		ingredients	
easy	250 g/9 oz rice noodles	4 tbsp sesame oil
	90 g/3¼ oz peanuts, chopped roughly	4 garlic cloves, crushed
serves 4		2 carrots, peeled and grated roughly
	3 tbsp fresh lime juice	2 eggs, beaten
	3 tbsp tomato ketchup	6 spring onions, sliced finely
12 minutes +20 minutes to soak noodles	1 tbsp light muscovado sugar	100 g/3½ oz fresh beansprouts
	2 tbsp soy sauce	
	1 tsp hot chilli sauce, or to taste	GARNISH
	250 g/9 oz firm tofu, cubed	2 limes, quartered
12 minutes	vegetable oil, for deep-frying	4 tbsp chopped fresh coriander

Soak the noodles in a bowl of warm water for about 20 minutes. Drain and set aside. In a small bowl, mix the peanuts, lime juice, ketchup, sugar, soy sauce and hot chilli sauce and set aside.

Put the noodles in boiling water and cook until the water starts to boil again. Remove, drain and set aside. Rinse the tofu, place between layers of kitchen paper and pat dry. Heat the vegetable oil in a pan and deep-fry the tofu on a medium heat for 2 minutes until light brown. Remove from the heat, lift out the tofu and set aside on kitchen paper to drain. Discard the vegetable oil.

Heat the sesame oil in the pan. Add the garlic and carrots and fry for 1 minute. Add the noodles and toss to coat. Add the peanut mixture and boil, stirring gently until the liquid is absorbed. Move the noodles to the side of the pan. Add the eggs, scramble, and mix with the noodles. Add the spring onions, beansprouts and tofu and stir-fry for 2 minutes. Remove from the heat, garnish and serve.

stir-fried asparagus & oyster mushrooms

		ingredients	
extremely easy		500 g/1 lb 2 oz asparagus, cut into 2.5 cm/1 inch pieces	pinch of chilli flakes
			salt and pepper, to taste
serves 4		125 ml/4 fl oz chicken stock	
		1 tbsp cornflour	GARNISH
		1 tbsp water	1 tbsp chopped fresh parsley
		2 tbsp vegetable oil	1 tsp chopped fresh chives
8 minutes		250 g/9 oz oyster mushrooms, sliced thinly	
10 minutes			

Steam the asparagus for 4–6 minutes until tender and set aside. Combine the chicken stock, cornflour and water in a small bowl and set aside.

Heat the oil in a large frying pan or wok over a medium heat. Stir-fry the asparagus, mushrooms and chilli flakes for 1–2 minutes. Stir in the chicken stock and bring to the boil. Reduce the heat, add the cornflour mixture and cook, stirring constantly for 2–3 minutes until thick.

Remove from the heat. Season to taste, garnish with the parsley and chives and serve immediately.

red cabbage & green beans

		ingredients
	extremely easy	250 g/9 oz fine green beans
		1 tsp sesame oil
	serves 4 (as a side dish)	1 onion, chopped finely
		3 carrots, cut into batons
		½ head red cabbage, shredded
	8 minutes	5 tbsp vegetable stock
		2 tbsp soy sauce
	14 minutes	

Boil a pan of water and blanch the green beans for 2–3 minutes. Remove from the heat, drain and plunge into ice-cold water.

In a large frying pan or wok, heat the oil and stir-fry the onion for 2 minutes. Add the carrots and cook for 3 minutes. Then mix in the green beans and stir-fry for 2 minutes. Finally, add the red cabbage and cook for 2 more minutes.

Pour in the vegetable stock and bring to the boil. Reduce the heat, cover and simmer for 3–4 minutes. Add the soy sauce.

Transfer to warm dishes and serve immediately.

garlic spinach

		ingredients	
	extremely easy	6 tbsp vegetable oil	1 tsp chilli sauce, or to taste
		6 garlic cloves, crushed	2 tbsp lemon juice
	serves 4 as a side dish	2 tbsp black bean sauce	salt and pepper
		3 tomatoes, chopped roughly	
		900 g/2 lb spinach, destalked and chopped roughly	
	6 minutes		
	4 minutes		

In a large frying pan or wok, heat the oil and stir-fry the garlic, black bean sauce and tomatoes for 1 minute. Stir in the spinach, chilli sauce and lemon juice and mix well. Cook for 3 minutes or until the spinach is just wilted. Season to taste.

Remove from the heat and serve immediately.

stir-fried broccoli

		ingredients	
	extremely easy	2 tbsp vegetable oil	1 tsp grated fresh root ginger
		2 medium heads of broccoli,	1 garlic clove, crushed
	serves 4 as a side dish	cut into florets	pinch of hot chilli flakes
		2 tbsp soy sauce	
		1 tsp cornflour	1 tsp toasted sesame seeds,
	8 minutes	1 tbsp caster sugar	to garnish
	8 minutes		

In a large frying pan or wok, heat the oil until almost smoking. Stir-fry the broccoli for 4–5 minutes.

In a small bowl, combine the soy sauce, cornflour, sugar, ginger, garlic and hot chilli flakes. Add the mixture to the broccoli. Cook over a gentle heat, stirring constantly, for 2–3 minutes until the sauce thickens slightly.

Transfer to a serving dish, garnish with the sesame seeds and serve immediately.

aubergine stir-fry

		ingredients	
very easy	2 aubergines		½ tsp paprika
	3 tbsp vegetable oil		¼ tsp ground cumin
serves 4 (as a side dish)	1 head of broccoli, cut into florets		3 tbsp water
	3 tomatoes, chopped roughly		2 tbsp chopped fresh coriander,
6 minutes +20 minutes to prepare aubergine	1 tsp salt		to garnish
12 minutes			

Trim the aubergines and cut into 2.5 cm/1 inch cubes. Place in a bowl, sprinkle with salt and set aside for 20 minutes to remove any bitter juices. Rinse and drain thoroughly.

In a frying pan or wok, heat 2 tablespoons of the oil until it is nearly smoking. Add the aubergine and stir-fry for 2–3 minutes. Remove from the heat and transfer to kitchen paper using a slotted spoon.

Heat the remaining tablespoon of oil in the pan and stir-fry the broccoli over a medium heat for 2–3 minutes. Add the tomatoes and salt and cook for a further 2 minutes. Stir in the paprika, cumin, water and cooked aubergine and mix together thoroughly. Reduce the heat, cover the pan and simmer for 5 minutes.

Remove from the heat, garnish with the coriander and serve.

index